AS THE BEAVER

Joel Drake Johnson

BROADWAY PLAY PUBLISHING INC
New York
www.broadwayplaypublishing.com
info@broadwayplaypublishing.com

AS THE BEAVER

Cover art by Larry B Salzmann
First printing: June 2010
I S B N: 978-0-88145-432-1

Book design: Marie Donovan
Page make-up: Adobe InDesign
Typeface: Palatino
Printed and bound in the U S A

ABOUT THE AUTHOR

Joel Drake Johnson is one of the newest members
of Chicago's Victory Gardens Theater Playwrights
Ensemble. The critically acclaimed, Jeff nominated
FOUR PLACES was produced by Victory Gardens in
the spring of 2008. His earlier works at V G, BEFORE
MY EYES and THE END OF THE TOUR, were also
Jeff-nominated for Best New Play and all three plays
were directed by Sandy Shinner, Victory Gardens'
Associate Artistic Director.

Johnson has won three Illinois Arts Council grants
including one for A BLUE MOON, which was
first produced at Chicago Dramatists and also Jeff
nominated for best new work . He got his start as a
writer at Chicago's critically acclaimed Econo-Art
Theater, which (under the leadership of Lynn Baber,
Barb Reeder and Marc Silvia) produced such plays
as BEAUTIFUL DREAMER. His other plays include
AS THE BEAVER, first produced by Zebra Crossing,
and THE FALL TO EARTH which premiered at
Steppenwolf Theater and featured Tony Award
Winner Rondi Reed. It was subsequently produced
at The Penguin Rep, directed by Joe Brancato and
featuring Tony Award Winner, Michelle Pawk.
Steppenwolf later produced A BLAMELESS LIFE and
TRANQUILLITY WOODS as part of their 2005 and
2007 First Look Repertory.

He has taught playwriting at Northwestern University, DePaul University and Stevenson High School in Lincolnshire. He lives in Chicago and New Buffalo, Michigan where he is working on three new plays: THE FIRST GRADE which was produced by the Aurora Theater Company in the winter of 2010; A GUIDE FOR THE PERPLEXED which will be produced by Victory Gardens in the summer of 2010 and will star Kevin Anderson and Fran Guinan; THE BOYS ROOM, first developed at Victory Gardens and later a part of Northlight Theater's Interplay and Steppenwolf Theater's First Look reading series.

Johnson is a member of The Dramatists Guild and Pen America.

Plays:

AS THE BEAVER, 1994, published by Broadway Play Publishing Inc
BEFORE MY EYES, 1998
A BLUE MOON, 2002
THE END OF THE TOUR, 2003, published by Broadway Play Publishing Inc
THE FALL TO EARTH, 2004, published by Broadway Play Publishing Inc
A BLAMELESS LIFE, 2005, Steppenwolf Theater commission
TRANQUILLITY WOODS, 2006, Steppenwolf Theater commission
THE FIRST GRADE, 2007, Steppenwolf Theater Commission and Aurora Theater GAP Playwrighting Award
FOUR PLACES, 2008, published by Northwestern University Press
A GUIDE FOR THE PERPLEXED, 2008, Aurora Theater GAP Playwrighting Award
THE BOYS ROOM, 2009, Victory Gardens 2011

ABOUT THE AUTHOR

Joel Drake Johnson is one of the newest members of Chicago's Victory Gardens Theater Playwrights Ensemble. The critically acclaimed, Jeff nominated FOUR PLACES was produced by Victory Gardens in the spring of 2008. His earlier works at V G, BEFORE MY EYES and THE END OF THE TOUR, were also Jeff-nominated for Best New Play and all three plays were directed by Sandy Shinner, Victory Gardens' Associate Artistic Director.

Johnson has won three Illinois Arts Council grants including one for A BLUE MOON, which was first produced at Chicago Dramatists and also Jeff nominated for best new work . He got his start as a writer at Chicago's critically acclaimed Econo-Art Theater, which (under the leadership of Lynn Baber, Barb Reeder and Marc Silvia) produced such plays as BEAUTIFUL DREAMER. His other plays include AS THE BEAVER, first produced by Zebra Crossing, and THE FALL TO EARTH which premiered at Steppenwolf Theater and featured Tony Award Winner Rondi Reed. It was subsequently produced at The Penguin Rep, directed by Joe Brancato and featuring Tony Award Winner, Michelle Pawk. Steppenwolf later produced A BLAMELESS LIFE and TRANQUILLITY WOODS as part of their 2005 and 2007 First Look Repertory.

He has taught playwriting at Northwestern University, DePaul University and Stevenson High School in Lincolnshire. He lives in Chicago and New Buffalo, Michigan where he is working on three new plays: THE FIRST GRADE which was produced by the Aurora Theater Company in the winter of 2010; A GUIDE FOR THE PERPLEXED which will be produced by Victory Gardens in the summer of 2010 and will star Kevin Anderson and Fran Guinan; THE BOYS ROOM, first developed at Victory Gardens and later a part of Northlight Theater's Interplay and Steppenwolf Theater's First Look reading series.

Johnson is a member of The Dramatists Guild and Pen America.

Plays:

AS THE BEAVER, 1994, published by Broadway Play Publishing Inc
BEFORE MY EYES, 1998
A BLUE MOON, 2002
THE END OF THE TOUR, 2003, published by Broadway Play Publishing Inc
THE FALL TO EARTH, 2004, published by Broadway Play Publishing Inc
A BLAMELESS LIFE, 2005, Steppenwolf Theater commission
TRANQUILLITY WOODS, 2006, Steppenwolf Theater commission
THE FIRST GRADE, 2007, Steppenwolf Theater Commission and Aurora Theater GAP Playwrighting Award
FOUR PLACES, 2008, published by Northwestern University Press
A GUIDE FOR THE PERPLEXED, 2008, Aurora Theater GAP Playwrighting Award
THE BOYS ROOM, 2009, Victory Gardens 2011

The first staged reading of AS THE BEAVER was on 31 October 1992 at Chicago Dramatists Workshop (Ross Tutterow, Artistic Director). The cast and creative conributor were:

THEODORE .... Rob Bundy
JUNE .... Annabel Armour
WARD .... John S Green
WALLY .... Rick Delaney
LITTLE RICKY .... David DeCastro
LUCY RICARDO .... Rebecca Borter
RICKY RICARDO .... Robert Andrew White
OPIE TAYLOR .... Randy Snyder
EDDIE HASKELL .... Richard Marlatt
MRS MAGILLICUTTY .... Lynne DuFresne

Director .... Ross Tutterow

AS THE BEAVER premiered at Zebra Crossing Theater in Chicago, Illinois on 17 January 1994 (Artistic Director, Marlene Zuccaro; Producing Director, Bob Buckwinkler). The cast and creative contributors were:

THEODORE (THE BEAVER)............................Joel Sugerman
JUNE... Ann James
WARD ....Michael Lomenick
WALLY..Robin M MacDuffie
LITTLE RICKY.. John Bukovec
RICKY RICCARDO .... Russell Alan Rowe
LUCY RICCARDO/MR ED .... Tucker Brown
MRS MAGILLICUTTY/REVEREND BEASLEY/
    JOHNNY JESSE RIVERS .... Sherman Shoemaker
OPIE TAYLOR..Scott Olson
EDDIE HASKELL .... John Bukovec

Director... Timber Weiss
Costume designer.............................Michele Friedman Siler
Lighting designer.. Jeff Childs
Set designer.. Tim Morrison
Production manager ....Le-ah Griffith
Graphic designer .... Mark Guarino
Sound designer... Timber Weiss

On 16 March 1994, this production was extended and reopened at The Theater Building in Chicago.

CHARACTERS & SETTING

JUNE
WARD
THEODORE, THE BEAVER
WALLY
LITTLE RICKY
RICKY RICCARDO
LUCY RICCARDO
OPIE TAYLOR
JOHNNY JESSE RIVERS
REVEREND BEASLEY
MR ED
EDDIE HASKELL
MRS MAGILLICUTTY

Several roles may be double cast

*The Cleaver home and surrounding area. Rerun Time. Check
Local Listings*

Special thanks to Larry B Salzmann

(*Halloween 1966. The kitchen of the Cleaver home.* LUCY *and* JUNE *are standing in the kitchen wearing their costumes. They are both dressed as pirates.*)

JUNE: Help me with this, Lucy. The boys will be here in a minute and I want the costume to look complete.

LUCY: (*As she helps* JUNE) Do you have any idea what they're wearing?

JUNE: I don't know, but they've been huddling secretly all day.

LUCY: I can't get a word out of Ricky.

JUNE: They think they're going to win first prize at the Country Club Halloween Ball, I know that.

LUCY: What do you suppose—

WARD: (*Offstage*) Alright girls, close your eyes.

RICCARDO: (*Off/thick Cuban accent*) You're about to see the animous decision of the judges!!!

LUCY: Come on, Ricky. Let us see.

RICCARDO: Close your eyes!

LUCY: Ricky!

RICCARDO: Better yet, shut off the lights!

LUCY: Oh, for heaven sake.

JUNE: Lets humor them, Lucy.

LUCY: Oh, all right.

(JUNE *turns off the light.*)

JUNE: You can come out now, boys!

(*In the dark, we can hear* WARD *and* RICCARDO *coming out, stumbling as they do.*)

RICCARDO: Hey, watch it, Cleaver.

WARD: You're the one who wanted the lights out.

LUCY: Like a couple of children.

JUNE: I guess.

RICCARDO: Okay, you can turn on the lights!

(*Lights go on and huge reaction from Lucy and June who laugh hysterically at the costumes of* RICCARDO *and* WARD. RICCARDO *is dressed as a Spanish princess and* WARD *is dressed as her duenna.*)

JUNE: Oh my gosh!!

LUCY: Ricky!

RICCARDO: (*Dancing*) La Cuccaracha! La Cuccaracha!

WARD: Who's going to win the first prize this year!

JUNE: (*Over* RICCARDO's *singing*) You are, dear!!!

(WALLY *and* EDDIE *come in.*)

EDDIE: Hey, Wally, your father's dressed like a woman.

WARD: How do you like my costume, Wally?

WALLY: Gee, Dad, I don't know.

RICCARDO: It will be the first prize in the contest tonight.

WALLY: Well, at least, you'll get something for it.

WARD: June, I don't think Wally approves of my costume.

LUCY: I think they're hilarious.

JUNE: Why don't I get the Beaver to see?

LUCY: And Little Ricky.

JUNE: Allright.

RICCARDO: We'll be singing out to the car. *(To* LUCY*)* Lets go you handsome devil!

LUCY: Oh Ricky!

(They dance out the door as RICCARDO *starts singing* La Cuccaracha *again and forces Lucy to dance with her. They all laugh and sing as lights fade to* THEODORE's *bedroom .* THEODORE *and* RICKY *lie on the bed.)*

THEODORE: You ever look at *Playboy* magazines?

RICKY: Sometimes.

THEODORE: You want to look at one now?

RICKY: You've got some?

THEODORE: Underneath the rug.

RICKY: Lets see.

*(*THEODORE *reaches under the bed.)*

THEODORE: I got Wally to buy this for me. Wait until you see.

(He opens up to the centerfold.)

RICKY: Wow! WOW!

THEODORE: Look at those tits.

RICKY: WOW!!

THEODORE: You know what I like to do?

RICKY: What?

THEODORE: Watch. *(He kisses the picture.)*

RICKY: WOW!

THEODORE: If I shut my eyes tight, I can feel them.

RICKY: You can't.

THEODORE: I can. Try it.

RICKY: Give me another page.

(THEODORE *turns the page.*)

THEODORE: Kiss that one.

(RICKY *does.*)

THEODORE: See what I mean?

RICKY: Wow, its great.

THEODORE: Are you getting a hard on?

RICKY: A what?

THEODORE: A boner.

RICKY: What's that?

THEODORE: Is your thing getting hard?

RICKY: What thing?

THEODORE: *(Indicating)* This thing!

RICKY: Oh, yeh. It is.

THEODORE: You want to take it out?

RICKY: Take it out?

THEODORE: And get it off.

RICKY: No.

THEODORE: Come on, it's fun.

RICKY: I don't want to.

THEODORE: We can lie here and jack each other off.

RICKY: I don't want to do that.

THEODORE: Do you even know what it is?

RICKY: I know what it is.

THEODORE: It feels great.

RICKY: I don't think I should.... What's it feel like anyway?

THEODORE: Like the best feeling in the world.

RICKY: It does?

THEODORE: Yeh.

RICKY: I think I hear my mom calling me.

THEODORE: Your mom's downstairs and she's not calling you.

RICKY: I'm going to go.

THEODORE: But you're supposed to spend the night with me.

RICKY: Listen, Beav. I don't think we ought to be talking this way. I don't feel right doing it.

THEODORE: Please.

RICKY: No.

THEODORE: I think I'm in love with you.

RICKY: You can't be.

THEODORE: I am. I think about you all the time. I think about us being naked—

RICKY: I'm getting out of here.

THEODORE: Kiss me and see if you don't like it.

RICKY: I won't.

THEODORE: Please. Just once.

RICKY: No way.

THEODORE: I think you'll like it.

RICKY: I don't—

THEODORE: Do you get excited when you see Little Joe on *Bonanza*?

RICKY: Well—

THEODORE: What about Paul McCartney of the Beatles?

RICKY: He's...

THEODORE: What about Mister Larocco, our gym teacher?

(RICKY *laughs.*)

RICKY: Or Marlon Brando?

THEODORE: Those arms!

RICKY: Those pecs!

(*Beat. They look at one another and then giggle. Beat*)

RICKY: Okay. Lets try it.

(RICKY *and* THEODORE *kiss.*)

THEODORE: What do you think?

RICKY: Lets try it again.

(RICKY *and* THEODORE *kiss again. This time, it is long and deep.*)

RICKY: Maybe I'm in love with you, too, Beav.

THEODORE: You think so?

RICKY: Maybe.

(RICKY *and* THEODORE *kiss again.*)

THEODORE: Oh Wow! Oh Wow! This is the best thing that's ever happened to me!

RICKY: Shhhhh.

(RICKY *and* THEODORE *kiss again. As* THEODORE *wraps his arms around* RICKY, JUNE —*in full costume—comes in.*)

JUNE: Beaver!!

(*Both* RICKY *and* THEODORE *stop.*)

RICKY: He made me!

JUNE: Ward! Get up here right away!

RICKY: He made me do it!

JUNE: You both stay right there.

RICKY: I gotta go. I hear my mom calling.

JUNE: (*Running to door*) WARD!

THEODORE: Mom—

JUNE: Go sit on the bed. And you, sit on Wally's bed.

THEODORE: We weren't doing anything.

JUNE: You were kissing.

RICKY: I wasn't kissing back.

THEODORE: Yes, you were.

JUNE: Boys do not kiss. Ward! Come upstairs please.

(WARD *comes in.*)

WARD: What is all the racket?

THEODORE: We weren't doing anything, Dad.

(WALLY *and* EDDIE *come in.*)

WALLY: What did you do, Beav?

JUNE: Wally, get downstairs.

WALLY: What are you yelling at me for?

WARD: What happened, June?

JUNE: When I opened the door, Theodore and Little Ricky were kissing.

EDDIE: Hey, Wally, your little brother is a fag.

WARD: Eddie, I think you'd better go home now.

EDDIE: Oh sure, Mister Cleaver. Do you want me to shut the door for you?

JUNE: Yes, Eddie. You can shut the door.

EDDIE: And don't worry, Mrs Cleaver. I won't tell anyone.

WARD: Wally, I think you had better leave as well.

WALLY: Boy, Beav, are you in trouble now.

(WALLY *and* EDDIE *leave.*)

WARD: I think, June, that maybe you should ask Lucy and Riccardo to come up.

RICKY: No! My parents will kill me.

WARD: Go ahead, June.

RICKY: *(Crying)* I didn't do anything. He made me.

(JUNE opens the door. WALLY and EDDIE fall into the room.)

JUNE: Wally!

WARD: *(Nearly loosing his temper)* Wally, you get out of this house and take that dip you call a friend with you!

WALLY: Dad!

EDDIE: Dip?

WARD: *(Calmly)* Wally, leave the room.

WALLY: *(As he leaves)* Geez, it's not me that's queer.

EDDIE: *(Going with WALLY)* Yeh, and your father wears a dress.

JUNE: *(As they move to the kitchen)* Get down those stairs.

EDDIE: Yes, Mrs Cleaver. Sorry, Mrs Cleaver.

JUNE: *(In kitchen)* As soon as your father and I are through with the Beaver, you're to take some of your things out of the room and sleep in the study.

WALLY: Why—

JUNE: Don't argue with me, Wally. Just do it.

(She goes out as crossfade to bedroom. Pause. WARD, THEODORE, and RICKY remain in the room.)

WARD: So what were you doing, Theodore?

THEODORE: Nothing.

WARD: Your mother says you were kissing Little Ricky.

(Beat)

WARD: Were you kissing Little Ricky?

RICKY: He was, but I wasn't kissing back.

WARD: Why were you kissing Little Ricky?

(*Beat*)

RICKY: Because he said he loved me.

WARD: Is that true, Theodore?

THEODORE: Yes.

WARD: You love Little Ricky?

THEODORE: Yes.

WARD: Do you know it's wrong for you to love Little Ricky?

THEODORE: Yes, but I can't help it, Dad. Nothing I do makes me stop feeling the way I do. I look at *Playboy* magazines because I think that will help, but it doesn't.

WARD: Maybe you'd better go, Little Ricky.

RICKY: Okay.

(*Much noise from hallway*)

RICKY: It's Mom and Dad. They're going to kill me.

LUCY: (*As the* RICCARDOS *enter.*) Now Ricky! Now Ricky!

RICCARDO: Where is he? Little Ricky! Little Ricky!

WARD: He's under the bed.

LUCY: Now Ricky, what are you going to do?

RICCARDO: (*Dragging* RICKY) I am going to beat him until he is blue and black. Stand up there! Stand up!

RICKY: I didn't do anything, Dad.

RICCARDO: You were kissing a boy!

RICKY: I didn't kiss back!

THEODORE: Yes, you did.

(RICCARDO *slaps* RICKY *across the face.*)

LUCY: Ricky!

RICCARDO: You stay out of this! (*Shaking* RICKY) Why did you kiss him? Why would do that?

JUNE: Ward, do something!

WARD: Listen, Riccardo—

RICCARDO: And you can just stay out of this, too, Cleaver!! I've never liked you or your wife or sons— who is full homosexuality and a sissy like his father!

JUNE: WARD!

LUCY: Now calm down, Ricky!

RICCARDO: I won't calm down. (*To* RICKY) And when I get home—

(RICCARDO *grabs* RICKY *and starts hitting him again.* LUCY *jumps on top of* RICCARDO *and tries to stop him. There is much yelling and screaming and crying as all parties try to stop the melee. The* I Love Lucy *theme song plays during this as the lights fade and then black out. Lights come up on the kitchen.* WALLY *and* EDDIE.)

EDDIE: So what are you going to do, Wally?

WALLY: What do you mean?

EDDIE: Your brother's a queer.

WALLY: You really think he is?

EDDIE: I've thought so all along. He's always biting his nails.

WALLY: I didn't know that meant you were queer.

EDDIE: Boy, are you dumb.

WALLY: But a lot guys bite their nails.

EDDIE: So they got to have that right combination.

WALLY: What do you mean?

EDDIE: If they bite their nails, they gotta be good at sports and really dig up on the girls or something, or not read a lot of books. Otherwise, they're faggots.

WALLY: How do you know this stuff, Eddie?

EDDIE: I got queer radar. My dad taught it to me right off when I was a little kid. And he always said that if you spot a queer, you gotta be careful about bending over, because they always want to poke you when you bend over. You ever see me bend over in the showers when Lumby is in class?

WALLY: No.

EDDIE: That's because Lumby is queer.

WALLY: He is? But he's such a nice guy.

EDDIE: He'd poke you in the butt if you bent over. Faggots just can't help themselves.

WALLY: Wow.

(*Lots of noise as* LUCY, RICKY *and* RICCARDO *come through the kitchen.*)

RICCARDO: (*Pushing* RICKY) Get on home! Go!

LUCY: Don't do that, Ricky! Ricky!

RICCARDO: He goes to Cuba! To Cuba!

LUCY: No, Ricky!

RICCARDO: There will not be no faggots in my house! No faggots, Lucy! In Cuba, they teach him how to be a man or he stands before a firing squad!!

LUCY: Ricky!

(*They exit.*)

EDDIE: Wow, they're going to shoot their own son. My dad says all queers should be shot through the head. They should be rounded up like cattle with hoof and mouth disease, and then shot. Boy, would I like to see something like that! Hey! I've got an idea. Lets go look through the windows of the Riccardo house and see what they're going to do. Maybe we'll witness a murder and then we can turn it in and be heroes or something.

WALLY: I don't want to witness a murder.

EDDIE: You a faggot like your brother?

(WALLY *grabs* EDDIE *as if to hit him.*)

WALLY: My brother is not a faggot.

EDDIE: Okay, alright. Then lets go watch Mister Riccardo murder his son. *(He starts to go.)* Come on.

(EDDIE *exits. Beat. Then* WALLY *follows. Cross-fade to bedroom. Silence. Then)*

WARD: Do you have anything to say, Beaver?

THEODORE: No.

(*Silence as* JUNE *whispers in* WARD's *ear.*)

WARD: Do you realize how serious this is?

THEODORE: Yes.

(*Silence as* JUNE *whispers in* WARD's *ear.*)

WARD: What would you like to do about it?

THEODORE: I don't know.

(*Silence as* JUNE *whispers in* WARD's *ear.*)

WARD: Do you know it's illegal for a boy to kiss another boy?

THEODORE: No.

WARD: *(To* JUNE*)* Are you sure...

(JUNE *whispers in* WARD's *ear.*)

WARD: You can't do that sort of thing, Beaver. It's not right.

(*Silence as* JUNE *whispers in* WARD's *ear—ever more rapidly.*)

WARD: People hate you when you do that sort of thing.

(*Silence as* JUNE *whispers in* WARD's *ear.*)

WARD: We don't understand you, Beaver.

(*Silence as* JUNE *whispers in* WARD's *ear.*)

WARD: And remember that as long as you are in our house, you do what we ask you to do.

(*They both exit and go downstairs.* THEODORE *sits up and looks around the room. He gets out of bed, takes off his clothes and then crawls under the covers, pulling the blanket over his head. Strains of the* Leave it to Beaver *theme plays. As the lights cross-fade to a spot on* WALLY *and* EDDIE*. In the background we can hear* LUCY *and* RICCARDO *talking in loud voices.*)

EDDIE: Oh wow, right to the kisser. Did you see that, Wally?

WALLY: Lets not do this anymore.

EDDIE: Now he's beating on Little Ricky and Little Ricky is just taking it! He's gotta be a fag. Now Mrs Riccardo is crying. She sure cries loud. Oh, wow, Mister and Mrs Brady just came in and Mister Brady is dragging Mister Riccardo off of Little Ricky. Oh my God, Mister Brady just ripped Mister Riccardo's dress and now Mister Riccardo is hysterical, pointing at the rip and crying and now beating on the floor! This is so much better than T V. This is even better than watching Annette take off her clothes in front of the window.

(WALLY *has left.*)

EDDIE: Hey, Wally! Wally! You're missing the action!!

(*Crossfade to kitchen.* JUNE *and* WARD*. She is busying herself with mindless cleaning. There is silence. Then*)

WARD: (*Good spiritedly as* JUNE *listens.*) You know this reminds me of the time when I was a teenager. You remember Andy Hardy, Judge Hardy's son? Well, a bunch of us guys went to the dance after a football game and we saw ole' Andy Hardy out there in the middle of the gym floor jitter bugging up a storm with his cousin Judy and so we all sort of dared one another to go up to ole' Andy, who we always thought was sort of that way, and so each of one of us goes up to ole' Andy and says "Hey, Andy, you wanna dance?" and then we'd move back and all start laughing and then the next guy would go up and do the same thing and this kept up for, oh I don't know, awhile anyway. And Andy would look at us real shamed-faced and all until finally, Judy steps out and goes into this tirade about how we should all grow up and if we were half as decent a person as Andy Hardy the world would be a better place to live and everybody in the gym applauded her. And then she and Andy got out on the floor and did this incredible jitter bug number that just knocked everybody out, it's so great. I guess we all do stupid things when we're kids. *(He laughs to himself.)* He got killed in World War Two. *(He stops laughing.)* Andrew Hardy killed in action. I remember that. Killed in action. *(Beat)* What a bunch of creeps we were.

(MISTER ED *pops his head in the window.)*

WARD: Hello, Mister Ed.

MISTER ED: Hey, those are some costumes. I bet you win the Country Club prize tonight! What do you think of my costume?

WARD: Who are you, anyway?

MISTER ED: Elizabeth Taylor in *National Velvet.*

JUNE: That's a very nice riding hat, Mister Ed.

MISTER ED: Thank you. So what's this I hear flying all over town like a flock of horseflies.

JUNE: What are you hearing?

MISTER ED: That there's some sort of trouble between Beaver and the Riccardo boy.

JUNE: Don't believe half of what you hear, Mister Ed.

MISTER ED: I just wanted to check the old rumor mill. So it's not true?

WARD: There's been some—

JUNE: No, it's not true.

MISTER ED: Well, that's good to hear. When I was just a colt—

JUNE: We're very busy right now, Mister Ed.

MISTER ED: I can't tell you one story?

JUNE: Not right now.

MISTER ED: Well, then, maybe I'll just drop by the Riccardo house—

JUNE: That's a good idea.

MISTER ED: Well, you tell the Beav that I'm thinking of him and that I hope everything gets straighten out.

JUNE: Mister Ed?

MISTER ED: Yes?

JUNE: I want you to remember that there are children involved in this.

MISTER ED: I never speak unless I have something to say.

JUNE: You've got the biggest mouth in town and if I hear that you've told one person this story, I swear to God you'll be dog food for Lassie.

MISTER ED: Just because I'm a talking horse, doesn't make me the cause of all the problems around this town!!!

JUNE: I'm warning you!

WARD: She's very upset right now, Mister Ed.

MISTER ED: I can see that, but I've got one thing to say about that and then I'll leave. Your son didn't kill anybody, Mrs Cleaver. He didn't rob a store! He didn't hurt a soul! And that's about all I'm going to say!

(MISTER ED *leaves.*)

JUNE: Stupid horse.

WARD: Why do you always let him get to you?

JUNE: I don't know why, but he does.

WARD: We have enough problems.

JUNE: I won't take the blame for this, Ward.

WARD: No one is blaming you.

JUNE: They always blame this kind of thing on strong willed mothers. There was an article in the *Ladies Home Journal* and in that article, they said that homosexuality in children is the direct result of overbearing mothers. Have I been overbearing?

WARD: No.

JUNE: Has Beaver spent too much time with me?

WARD: No.

JUNE: He always helps me in the house while Wally always goes out to the garage with you. Why do you always do that?

WARD: What?

JUNE: Ask Wally to come out and help you, but never the Beaver?

WARD: Beaver never seemed interested.

JUNE: Maybe it you had asked him. And what do you do out in the garage every Saturday?

WARD: Exactly what you tell me to do.

JUNE: Well, maybe you ought to start taking the Beaver with you. I won't let him help me in the house anymore. Have you ever noticed how much he likes to dust? I never thought of it before, but isn't that just a little abnormal? Why haven't you ever said anything about it? The Beaver is sixteen now. It may be too late!

WARD: There's no point in blaming—

JUNE: *(Angry)* I'm going to blame someone! No one is going to point the finger at me. *(Stopping her activity)* He didn't go to prom this year.

WARD: What?

JUNE: The Beaver didn't go to the prom. I thought it was because he was too shy. I suggested to him that because he was a junior in high school and this was his first prom that he should ask Patty from next door and he said "I don't like Patty. She's too goofy." And I said why not her cousin, Cathy? and he said "She was stuck up." *(She cleans some more. Then stops.)* If I see that Lucy Riccardo again...

WARD: What?

JUNE: After what Ricky said to you?

WARD: I don't pay any attention to him.

JUNE: And who spilled this cranberry juice on the table. Was it you?

WARD: No.

JUNE: Because it is now a permanent stain. Right here in the middle of the table! Wally! Wally!

WARD: Don't start getting after Wally.

JUNE: He's a slob.

WALLY: *(Coming in)* Why is everybody yelling at me?

WARD: Nevermind son—

JUNE: Did you spill this juice on the table?

WALLY: I don't—

JUNE: Right here!

WARD: June—

JUNE: Now you've ruined the table!

WALLY: I never did it!

JUNE: Who did then? Your father??

(A dim light appears on THEODORE *who is listening at his door.)*

WALLY: I don't know, Mom.

JUNE: Why is it you can never tell the truth?

WALLY: I'm not a liar, Mom.

JUNE: And if you ever bring that disgusting Eddie Grundy in here again, I will take both him and you by the scruff of the neck—

WALLY: *(Near tears)* Mom!

JUNE: I've had it with him. "No, Mrs Cleaver. Yes, Mrs Cleaver."

WARD: *(Loudly)* All right! That's enough!

WALLY: Dad, I didn't do anything. Maybe I spilled the cranberry juice, maybe I did, I don't know. I don't remember!

WARD: It's okay, son.

WALLY: The Beaver does something wrong and everybody acts like they hate me.

WARD: *(Going to hug* WALLY*)* It's okay, Wally.

WALLY: Don't hug me!

WARD: Wally!

WALLY: *(Quietly)* I don't want to be hugged. *(Beat)* Mom. if I spilled the cranberry juice, I'm real sorry. And if the stain won't come out, I'll save money from my job at Miller's grocery to buy you another one. I just don't want you to hate me for it, that's all.

JUNE: I don't hate you, Wally. I love you.

(*Beat*)

WALLY: Do you hate the Beaver? He's a good kid, Mom.

JUNE: I know. I don't hate the Beaver.

WALLY: Why are you making me move out of the room?

WARD: What's that?

JUNE: I told Wally to sleep in the study tonight.

WARD: Well—

JUNE: We thought it would be best for the time being.

WALLY: He's not going to do anything to me, Dad. I don't think I can catch anything from him.

WARD: For the time being.

WALLY: The time being?

WARD: You know, Wally, there are time when people need to be alone.

WALLY: Like when you come home from a bad day at the office and then yell at me when I come into your study to ask for money?

JUNE: What your father means, Wally, is that there are certain things that a person can think over better when they are by themselves.

WALLY: Like when you yell at Dad for coming home late and then he slaps you across the face and you run to your bedroom crying and won't let anybody in for a whole day? (*Beat*) I'll go make my bed in the study.

JUNE: I'll come in later to help you.

WALLY: Thanks, Mom...Mom, Dad, is the Beaver going to be okay, do you think?

WARD: He'll be okay.

WALLY: That's good...I'm sorry if I yelled.

WARD: We know you are.

WALLY: Well, good night.

JUNE & WALLY: Good night, Wally.

(WALLY *leaves. Pause*)

WARD: I think we should see someone.

JUNE: What do you mean?

WARD: I think we should talk to Reverend Beasley.

JUNE: No.

WARD: June, we're going to need some help with this. I can call him tonight.

(*Beat*)

WARD: June?

JUNE: It's me, isn't it?

WARD: It's all of us.

(JUNE *begins to rub at the stain on table. She stops. Then*)

JUNE: Call him.

(*Lights cross-fade to* THEODORE's *bedroom.* WALLY *comes in.* THEODORE *lies on his bed.* WALLY *comes in and tiptoes to his bed. He takes off a pillow and a blanket and begins to leave.*)

WALLY: Beav? Beav?

THEODORE: What?

WALLY: How could you do it, Beav?

THEODORE: I don't want to talk about it.

(*Beat*)

WALLY: They're sending Little Ricky to a military school in Cuba. I guess Mister Riccardo gave it to Little Ricky really bad. Eddie says he has a black eye. (*Beat*)
WALLY: Hey, Beav?

THEODORE: I don't feel much like talking, Wally.

WALLY: Well, that's okay...hey, Beav?

THEODORE: What?

WALLY: Do you feel like it now?

THEODORE: What?

WALLY: That you like guys?

THEODORE: I'm not talking about that ever again. So just leave me alone.

WALLY: I was just wondering that when you get in a down mood if you still feel it. When I get in a down mood, I can hardly even think about it—even Peggy Josephsen and she's the cutest girl in the school...hey, Beav?

THEODORE: Yeh?

WALLY: Do you like all guys or just Little Ricky?

THEODORE: I don't want to talk about it.

WALLY: Okay.

THEODORE: And I don't like all guys. Eddie Grundy makes me sick.

(*Beat*)

WALLY: You know what I think, Beav?

THEODORE: What?

WALLY: That it will go away. In a couple of days or so or maybe a week like when we both had the measles and were so sick and wanted to throw up all the time. I think that's all it is.

THEODORE: *(Sitting up for the first time)* You think so, Wally?

WALLY: I'll bet so.

THEODORE: Yeh, maybe you're right.

WALLY: And when it goes away, Mom and Dad will let me come back in here to sleep.

THEODORE: They won't let you sleep in here?

WALLY: They said they thought it would be better and well, heck Beav, I told them I didn't think what you had was catching, but they're forcing me to do it.

(THEODORE lies back down.)

WALLY: Criminey, Beav, I don't want to do it. I mean, you're my brother and all, and you do stupid thing, but I like you.

THEODORE: Just go ahead, Wally. I don't care.

(Beat)

WALLY: Beaver?

THEODORE: Go away.

WALLY: Beaver, I just want to let you know that if you decide to run away, be sure to tell me, because I'll go with you.

THEODORE: You will?

WALLY: We're brothers, aren't we?

THEODORE: Gee, Wally, you're just about the best brother any guy ever had.

WALLY: There's nothing better I'd like to do than to get the fuck out of here.

(Beat. THEODORE and WALLY both laugh.)

WALLY: I'll see you later, Beav.

THEODORE: I'll see you later, Wally.

(THEODORE *and* WALLY *do a corny kind of handshake.*
WALLY *starts to go.*)

WALLY: And, Beav?

THEODORE: Yeh?

WALLY: I hope you're feeling better soon.

THEODORE: Thanks, Wally.

(WALLY *leaves. Crossfade to spot where* RICCARDO *and*
WARD *stand.*)

RICCARDO: Look at this dress! This was my mother's
dress from Cuba! Now it's ruined and I have no
peoples to blame but the curse of homosexuality. She is
turning in her grave as we speak and all she can do is
moan and chant her tears to the ground! Wasn't I man
enough? Wasn't I rough with Lucy? Didn't I act like the
cock of the road! Didn't he be see me this way? No one
in this family has ever been a sissy except for Cousin
Ramone who was crazy, thinking he was Carmen
Miranda and wearing a load of bananas in his pants,
but we beat him up and sent him to the assissylum.
And I never toodled with him, never except when I got
drunk and he would stick his butt out of the window!
What will I do, Cleaver?! What will I do if I have a sissy
son?

WARD: Share a wardrobe.

(*He walks away.*)

RICCARDO: This is no time for a joke! No time for a joke,
Cleaver!!

(*Crossfade to the kitchen.* LUCY, MRS MAGILLICUTTY *and*
JUNE *sit at the table.*)

LUCY: He just sits there, staring straight ahead.

MRS MAGILLICUTTY: He has a terrible black eye and a
bloody lip.

LUCY: His face is all swollen. I didn't think I could take him to the doctor, because they would ask questions. So we packed up a few things and we're moving into mother's place.

MRS MAGILLICUTTY: It's about time you got out of that Cuban hothouse.

LUCY: But you know what Little Ricky insisted on taking with him? His drum set. He said he had to keep practicing so that his dad would be proud of him. Can you imagine?

MRS MAGILLICUTTY: I told you not to marry Nickey.

LUCY: Ricky.

MRS MAGILLICUTTY: Exactly! All those Cubans are communist! Look at the Bay of Dogs.

LUCY: Pigs.

MRS MAGILLICUTTY: They are and that's for sure. Castro, communists and Cuba add up to just one thing and that's Ricky Riccardo!

LUCY: So I wanted to ask you if you would do me a favor?

JUNE: If I can.

LUCY: If Ricky comes over here looking for me, don't tell him where I went.

JUNE: Of course not.

MRS MAGILLICUTTY: If he comes near my house, I'll shoot him dead!

LUCY: Tell him you haven't seen me.

MRS MAGILLICUTTY: I've also got a few chickens I can throw at him.

LUCY: Mother, please! *(To* JUNE*)* I don't think I'll be back.

JUNE: Oh, no.

LUCY: And I wanted to say goodbye. You've been such a good friend.

JUNE: I'll miss you.

LUCY: Oh, me, too.

MRS MAGILLICUTTY: (As LUCY cries) Now, honey, things will be better.

JUNE: They will.

(MRS MAGILLICUTTY takes LUCY in her arms.)

MRS MAGILLICUTTY: (Singing)
Somewhere over the rainbow, bluebirds fly.

ALL THREE WOMEN: "Birds fly over the rainbow, why oh why can't I."

MRS MAGILLICUTTY: "If happy little bluebirds fly beyond the rainbow—

ALL: Why, oh why, can't I?"

(Short pause. We hear THEODORE singing a religious tune upstairs. It is very soft and low. They listen.)

JUNE: The Reverend Beasley is talking to the Beaver. He's missing the Country Club Ball just for this. He's wearing his Virgin Mary costume.

LUCY: I love him in that.

JUNE: Me, too.

(Beat)

LUCY: So do you think...

JUNE: What?

LUCY: That the Beaver and Little Ricky are...

JUNE: I don't think so.

LUCY: But if they are, will they blame us?

JUNE: I don't know, Lucy.

LUCY: I can't imagine what I did.

JUNE: I think it must be a phase.

LUCY: I think so, too.

MRS MAGILLICUTTY: My brother William went through a phase like that.

LUCY: Uncle Bill?

MRS MAGILLICUTTY: Lasted him all his life.

LUCY: Uncle Bill was a...

MRS MAGILLICUTTY: A poof? Yes, he was.

LUCY: But he was my favorite uncle.

MRS MAGILLICUTTY: And my favorite brother. Such a darling man. Sweetest soul. It made me wish that all men were poofs. He told wonderful stories, was very smart—

LUCY: I remember his stories.

MRS MAGILLICUTTY: He lived for years and years with that dear Miss Hathaway. People thought they were lovers living in sin, but they were like brother and sister. I was always envious of them both. Your father...well, like mother, like daughter as they say. But then, Miss Hathaway died of cancer. She smoked like a chimney. I remember saying "Jane dear, you just smoked a cigarette and you're having another?" She'd tell me to mind my own business—which I would—and then she'd light up another! The awful day of the funeral, I walked into Billy's bedroom where he lay crying on the bed, and I stroked his head and I remember the dye of his hair came off in my hands. My hand was black with dye and it made me doubly sad for him. Then he turned over and his face was puffy and red from crying, but I could see that he still had beautiful skin, very soft and pretty. I told your father straight out that if he didn't offer Uncle Bill a place in our home, he could darn well live the rest of his life without me and then who would cook his miserable breakfast in the morning! I hope Little Ricky is a poof, that's what I say. At least, we can be sure he'll be a decent and kind man!!

LUCY: Mother!

MRS MAGILLICUTTY: And wouldn't that put an end to football!!

LUCY: Mother, why don't you go out to the car.

MRS MAGILLICUTTY: *(Starting to leave)* Your father used to say "one in the hand is worth two in the bush" and I'd say right back to him "who cares what you think"!

LUCY: Mother.

MRS MAGILLICUTTY: Allrighty. *(She exits.)*

LUCY: She does go on, doesn't she? *(Beat)* I'll write to you, June. Now don't cry.

JUNE: I'm not crying.

LUCY: We girls just have to go on.

JUNE: I know.

LUCY: I love you.

JUNE: I love you.

(They hug. LUCY exits. Cross-fade to THEODORE's bedroom. Reverend BEASLEY and THEODORE sit on the bed singing A Mighty Fortress is Our God. *BEASLEY is dressed as the Virgin Mary.)*

BEASLEY: Very good! You have a very nice voice, Theodore. You should join the youth choir.

THEODORE: Thank you.

BEASLEY: There are lots of pretty girls in the choir. *(Beat)* BEASLEY: Now Theodore.

THEODORE: Yes, Reverend.

BEASLEY: Your parents have told me what happened today.

THEODORE: I know.

BEASLEY: They thought perhaps if you and I could talk, we might be able to solve your problem.

THEODORE: I don't mean to have a problem.

BEASLEY: I know you don't and that's why I'm here. To tell you that God loves you.

THEODORE: He does?

BEASLEY: He does not love your sin, he hates your sin, but he loves you.

THEODORE: Oh.

BEASLEY: Now I truly believe that if you want to be rid of the sin, you can and you will be. Do you want to be rid of the sin?

THEODORE: Yes.

BEASLEY: The Bible says that laying with another man is a sin. Did you know that, Theodore?

THEODORE: I felt it.

BEASLEY: Ahhh, then you are one step closer to being forgiven.

THEODORE: I want to be forgiven.

BEASLEY: Shall we ask God to take the sin away from you?

THEODORE: If you think that will work.

BEASLEY: Lets try that then. Shall we bow our heads in prayer?

(BEASLEY *and* THEODORE *do.*)

BEASLEY: Dear God, This boy who comes before you asks that you forgive him for his sin to you. He asks that you forgive and take from him this awful desire that has somehow crept into his soul. He asks you humbly, but with great, good resolve to serve you. He is only a child, God—how old are you, Theodore?

THEODORE: Sixteen.

BEASLEY: Almost a man, dear Lord, and he wants your understanding and your power to lift the crazed and immoral thoughts that filter through out and Out and OUT from within him. In Jesus Christ, we pray.

BEASLEY & THEODORE: Amen.

THEODORE: How long do you think it will take to work, Reverend?

BEASLEY: Well—

THEODORE: A longtime?

BEASLEY: I don't think that we can—

THEODORE: Because I can still feel it. I can tell that I'm the same.

BEASLEY: It would help for you to concentrate on other things.

THEODORE: It would?

BEASLEY: I think it would.

THEODORE: Oh. You only think it would?

BEASLEY: It will.

THEODORE: Oh.

BEASLEY: It is all up to you.

THEODORE: But I thought God would take it away.

BEASLEY: God helps those who help themselves.

THEODORE: But what if I don't know what to do?

BEASLEY: I just told you to concentrate.

THEODORE: What should I concentrate on? What would you concentrate on if you were like me?

BEASLEY: I would think about the pain I was causing my family.

THEODORE: Oh.

BEASLEY: I would think about the way you will be outcast in life.

THEODORE: Oh.

BEASLEY: I would think how impossible it will be to become a member of God's kingdom. I would also remind myself that every religion in the world— even the Jews and the Muslims—find homosexuality abhorrent and criminal and that some religions would rather have you dead than alive. That should be sufficient.

THEODORE: Oh... Am I breaking a commandment by being who I am?

BEASLEY: No. But it is still a sin.

THEODORE: Why isn't it a commandment?

BEASLEY: Because...I would suppose...it is a new sin.

THEODORE: But you said it was in the Bible.

BEASLEY: Yes, but no one had actually committed the sin.

THEODORE: Oh, I see. Where in the Bible does it say it is a sin?

BEASLEY: Right near the verse where it prohibits wearing garments made of two different kinds of yarns.

THEODORE: Oh. So if this feeling doesn't go away, I'll go to hell? Or possibly be killed?

BEASLEY: I can't speak for God, but you should pray to him daily until you have felt those feelings subside. *(Getting up to leave)* If you need my help, you should not hesitate to come see me.

THEODORE: All right...Reverend, do you hate me?

BEASLEY: Of course not.

THEODORE: But everyone else will. They do already.

BEASLEY: But once the sin has left you...

THEODORE: They'll like me again?

BEASLEY: Exactly. *(He turns to go.)*

THEODORE: Reverend Beasley, why aren't you married?

BEASLEY: I don't know what that has to do with—

THEODORE: You just haven't met the right woman, huh?

BEASLEY: If you mean to be disrespectful—

THEODORE: No.

BEASLEY: Then pray, Theodore.

(BEASLEY exits. THEODORE takes out paper and begins to write.)

THEODORE: July 30, 1966. Dear Ann Landers.
I am sixteen years old and a junior in high school and I do well in school and all, but when I walk down the hall or I'm in gym class, some of the guys call me a sissy or hit me hard in the arm. They call me a sissy because I am one. I have fantasies about guys if you know what I mean and today my mom caught me kissing one of the neighborhood boys. Now both my parents and my brother, Wally, hate me and don't want anything to do with me. I can hear my parents arguing and yelling at Wally and I know that it's all my fault. If I felt that maybe it would all go away, that I wouldn't like guys anymore, maybe then I'd be alright, but I have this terrible feeling that I'll always feel this way. And if I'm always like this then no one will like me and I'll be lonely all my life. I won't be able to marry and I won't have any kids and then what will

I do when I'm fifty years old and no one is around at
Christmas time? Please Mrs Landers, say something
in your column so that maybe if there is someone else
like me, they can feel better about it and or expect
it anyway or at least not kiss any boys because then
everybody knows about it and will hate you forever.
I apologize for my terrible handwriting, but I am very
upset right now.
Sincerely, Beaver.

(THEODORE *folds the letter up and sticks it in an envelope
and lays it on the bed. He goes out of the bedroom and into
the kitchen.* JUNE *is helping* WARD *remove his make-up.*)

THEODORE: Mom and Dad?

WARD & JUNE: Yes, Beaver?

THEODORE: It will never happen again. And I'm sorry
for getting you guys so upset.

JUNE: Oh, Beaver.

(JUNE *hugs* THEODORE.)

THEODORE: I'm going to get married and I'm going
to have two kids, a boy and a girl and the girl will be
named June and the boy will be named Ward.

WARD: Why, thank you, son.

THEODORE: Goodnight, Mom and Dad.

JUNE & WARD: Goodnight, Beaver.

(THEODORE *exits and goes to his room.*)

JUNE: Somehow I knew he'd pull through.

WARD: Now if we can just get him to clean his room.

(*Lights cross-fade to* THEODORE's *bedroom. He takes out
very thick rope and begins to tie it into a knot. As he does so,
he recites the Boy Scout Pledge.*)

THEODORE: On my honor I will do my best—To do my
duty to God and my country, and to obey the Scout

law; To help other people at all times; To keep myself physically strong, mentally awake, morally straight. *(By the time he has finished the pledge, he has fashioned a noose at the one end. He puts it around his neck, and then searches desperately for some place to hang the other end. Not able to find one)* I'm so stupid! I'm so stupid!

(Suddenly, he jumps up, ties the other end of the rope to the bed, opens his window, stands on the sill and jumps as the theme music from Leave it to Beaver *plays. Blackout)*

Scene Two

(In the dark, we hear a montage of commercials, music, and news reports that take us from 1966 to Halloween 1986. The lights come up on the same set which has changed only a little over the past twenty years. Lights come up on THEODORE's *bedroom. He and* OPIE *are putting on costumes that symbolize death. They are making posters that read Silence=Death, etc. They are very enthusiastic.)*

OPIE: *(Holding up a sign)* How does this look?

THEODORE: Great. Can you help me with this?

OPIE: *(As he helps* THEODORE *with costume)* So how do you think your parents are going to react?

THEODORE: Mom will be hysterical. Dad will get philosophical. The whole town will try to kill us without touching us. It'll be awful, but it will be worth it. How does it look?

OPIE: Very sexy.

THEODORE: How sexy?

OPIE: Turn on sexy.

THEODORE: So you're in love with death. That's nice to know.

OPIE: Kiss me.

THEODORE: I'll smear my lipstick.

OPIE: Then grab my crotch.

THEODORE: Ugly pervert.

(OPIE *gets* THEODORE *in a hug and they kiss.*)

THEODORE: You're creasing my buns.

OPIE: They'll spring back.

THEODORE: You start this, we'll never be ready.

OPIE: You're such a virgin now that you're home.

THEODORE: It's a hard thing to shake.

OPIE: So what do your parents think of me?

THEODORE: They hate your guts. You've turned their quiet, obedient, suicidal son into a radicalized seeker of life. They'd love to turn you out, but can't. They think you fuck me hard and that it makes me scream— which it does. They think you're an over-sexed, undernourished, homosexual mass murdering country boy who will leave their bodies rotting in a shallow grave.

(*Laughter from downstairs.*)

THEODORE: And they are—at this very minute— dressing themselves as Ron and Nancy Reagan so they can lead the Halloween Parade as grand marshalls and further demonstrate—in, oh, so subtle a way—the repulsion they feel for me, the disappointment that they hide, the shock and embarrassment that I can exist as I am after spending so many years in a terrible brainwash of fear and hatred and sterility.

OPIE: (*Applauding*) WOOOOOOOOOO!

THEODORE: Some funny speech, huh?

OPIE: Some funny speech.

THEODORE: When they catch a glimpse of us walking in the parade right behind them—

OPIE: Too cruel.

THEODORE: Too mean.

OPIE: Too fucking all right.

(OPIE *and* THEODORE *laugh as* JUNE *and* WARD *laugh downstairs. Lights cross-fade to kitchen.*)

JUNE: Do I look like Nancy Reagan?

WARD: Picture perfect. And me?

JUNE: I feel like I've fallen in love again.

(THEODORE *and* OPIE *laugh upstairs.*)

JUNE: What do you suppose they're doing?

WARD: Talking about us.

JUNE: And what do they say?

WARD: That we're boring middle-aged people.

JUNE: I don't like him, Ward.

WARD: Opie?

JUNE: Yes. He seems strange to me.

WARD: We talked about this.

JUNE: I know and I'm trying to be open-minded, but he wears his clothes too tight, he seems too muscular for a man his age, and he seems a little uncivilized. What is that accent, anyway? It makes me lock my bedroom door at night.

WARD: I've noticed.

JUNE: Well, I don't feel safe. And have you seen the change in Beaver? He's adopted a new look on his face. It makes me uncomfortable...I wish he would leave.

WARD: June—

JUNE: I do. I don't know him anymore. He moves away to a big city. We see him every two or three years and everytime he comes back, I have to stare at him for a minute before I recognize who he is.

WARD: How's this for a Reagan smile? (*He puts on a Reagan mask.*)

JUNE: Don't change the subject, Ward.

WARD: Ron.

JUNE: Please.

WARD: (*As Reagan*) We don't have a lot of time, Nancy.

(OPIE *and* THEODORE *laugh again.* JUNE *looks up.*)

JUNE: There it is again.

WARD: They can't laugh?

JUNE: They're doing something.

(*Beat*)

JUNE: I don't feel like we should do this. Not this year. Not with what has happened. Not with the way I feel. Wally going through a divorce—

WARD: We don't know that.

JUNE: Beaver looking pale and sickly and angrier than ever—

(*The horn honks.*)

WARD: There's the Riccardos now. Lets go.

JUNE: Go up and check on them, Ward.

WARD: They're grown men.

JUNE: Please. I'll go out to the car. (*She puts on her mask.*)

WARD: Did you take your medicine tonight?

JUNE: That is not—

WARD: Did you take it?

JUNE: Yes, I did.

(*The horn honks.*)

WARD: It won't look very good in the lead car if you're crying.

JUNE: I took the medicine, Ward. Now go up and check on the boys.

WARD: All right.

(WARD *goes up.* JUNE *goes to sink, gets a glass of water and downs her pills as lights fade to* THEODORE's *room.* THEODORE *stands at the window.*)

THEODORE: This is where I did it.

OPIE: What?

THEODORE: Tried to kill myself.

OPIE: Oh.

THEODORE: I wore a brace around my neck for six months. They sent me away—and for an entire year, I saw them once a month and we would talk or try to— and the room where we would meet was white with two windows not unlike these—and I would think, every time that they were there, I would think about those windows and what they were really used for—to get out, to get away, to kill oneself. Never to let in light, never to see. Never to look ahead.

(THEODORE *turns to* OPIE.)

THEODORE: I'm glad I met you.

OPIE: (*Extending his hand*) Death meets death.

THEODORE: Yes.

(*Beat*)

OPIE: My father locked me in the shed.

THEODORE: How awful.

OPIE: Not really. By that time, I liked the dark.

THEODORE: My parents had me talk to our minister.

OPIE: Mine, too.

THEODORE: Really?

OPIE: And when that didn't work, Pa whipped me and cried. Whack! and cry. Whack and cry. I love you he'd say. And Whack! and cry.

THEODORE: I love you.

(OPIE *begins to cry.*)

OPIE: I cannot stand thinking about it.

THEODORE: I love you. Think about that.

(*They embrace. Beat.*)

OPIE: So what if there's a riot?

THEODORE: We lay down in the streets.

OPIE: And get dragged off—

THEODORE: Kicking and screaming—

OPIE: "Til death do us part."

THEODORE: That's very good. "Til death do us part."

OPIE & THEODORE: We are your children and we're dying of AIDS!

(OPIE *and* THEODORE *begin to chant and march about the room as* WARD *comes to door. He stands outside and listens. Then knocks*)

THEODORE: Who is it?

WARD: It's your father, Beaver. Can I come in?

THEODORE: Not right now.

(*Beat*)

WARD: Well...is everything okay?

THEODORE: Everything is fine.

WARD: Good. Your mother and I are leaving.

THEODORE: Okay, have a great time.

WARD: Are you coming down to the parade?

THEODORE: Yes. Eventually. Opie and I have a few things to finish up.

WARD: You do?

THEODORE: Just a few things.

(*Beat*)

WARD: Would you and Opie like to come to the Country Club Ball after the parade?

(OPIE *and* THEODORE *look at one another.*)

THEODORE: I don't think so.

OPIE: Thanks for the invite.

WARD: Was that Opie?

THEODORE: Yes.

WARD: You're welcome, Opie.

(*The horn honks.*)

THEODORE: Sounds like you better go, Dad.

(*Beat*)

WARD: All right...see you at the parade!

(*He exits. They listen for him to leave. Then*)

THEODORE: Thank God. Are you ready?

OPIE: For a blow job.

THEODORE: (*Kissing him*) Soon as we make our getaway. Lets go.

(*Music as* OPIE *and* THEODORE *steal out the door. Blackout. Then sirens, sounds of banging and clanging. Lights up on kitchen.* JUNE, WARD, LUCY, *and* RICCARDO *run into the kitchen.*)

JUNE: I can't stand this! I can't stand this!!

WARD: June—

JUNE: The humiliation.

LUCY: Lets not overreact.

RICCARDO: A more pathetical sight I hope to never see!

LUCY: Are you trying to make it worse?

RICCARDO: That boy should have been sent to the remortuary!!

JUNE: I can't go out of this house again.

RICCARDO: She has negagofobia!

WARD: No one knew who they were.

LUCY: Of course not.

RICCARDO: I knew right away it was the Beaver.

LUCY & WARD: Shut up!

JUNE: *(Going to sink for more pills)* But he did it to us, to us. Why?

(MISTER ED *sticks his head in the window.)*

MISTER ED: That was some commotion down at the parade.

LUCY: This is not a good time to be here, Mister Ed.

MISTER ED: Rumor has it that it was your son, Beaver—

WARD: Mister Ed, why don't you go back to your stable?

MISTER ED: Who would have ever dreamed it?

LUCY: Mister Ed, please.

MISTER ED: They say the Beaver has AIDS.

JUNE: What?

WARD: Mister Ed, who's ever spreading that around—

MISTER ED: He said it when he was arrested. They both did. Said they both had AIDS and were disrupting the parade because they were sick of the way bougersoise America was systematically killing them off. Never thought I'd see the day when little Beaver would be using such big words. Made me proud of him.

JUNE: I can't believe it.

MISTER ED: I just thought you knew.

JUNE: We didn't know, Mister Ed

MISTER ED: Well, I'm sorry. I...

WARD: Don't you think you ought to leave now, Mister Ed.

MISTER ED: I suppose. I'm really sorry. I'm sorry for all of you. Theodore is a good boy, a good man, a good person. He doesn't deserve this. And although I've been in the closet now for many years, dating one filly after another—

LUCY: Mister Ed!

MISTER ED: I am proud to say that today, yes, I am a gay horse!! God bless the Beaver!

(*A stunned silence*)

MISTER ED: If you need anything, you let me know... Good night.

(*He leaves. Pause. Then*)

RICCARDO: I will never ride that horse again!

(*All look at* RICCARDO *who suddenly realizes what he has said. Beat.* JUNE *hangs her head.*)

WARD: June...

JUNE: Well...

WARD: June, honey...

JUNE: So he came home to die, did he? That's what I call the perfect ending.

(*Siren sounds once again until suddenly the lights flash on to reveal* EDDIE *and* RICKY *as policeman, surrounding* THEODORE *who still wears his outfit and is sitting in a chair as if he is being questioned.*)

THEODORE: Where's Opie?

EDDIE: So you were walking down—

THEODORE: Where's Opie?

EDDIE: You were walking down the street—

THEODORE: I want to know where Opie is—

EDDIE: In another cell. You think we'd put two fags in the same room together? You think we're nuts? (*Beat*) So you were walking down the middle of the street, hey Beav?

THEODORE: I was walking down the street, hey Eddie.

EDDIE: Asshole.

THEODORE: Yeh, okay. So throw me in jail for the night.

EDDIE: What is this shit you've got on?

THEODORE: A costume. It's Halloween, isn't it?

EDDIE: So what kind of faggoty shit is this all about?

THEODORE: It's too ward off ignorant breeders like yourself.

EDDIE: What?

THEODORE: Have any kids, Eddie?

EDDIE: I've got three—

THEODORE: Too bad.

EDDIE: What the hell—

THEODORE: Too fast for you, Eddie?

EDDIE: You don't know what I can do to you.

THEODORE: You've already done it. You're the winner. I'm the loser. Congratulations.

(Beat)

EDDIE: I'm gonna have to charge you, Beaver.

THEODORE: All right.

EDDIE: Disturbing the peace and inciting a riot. Keep an eye on him, Rick, while I do the paper work. *(He leaves.)*

THEODORE: So you don't say anything?

(Beat)

THEODORE: Weird. Very weird.

RICKY: I'm okay now, Beaver.

THEODORE: I see.

(Beat)

RICKY: I'm sorry you got AIDS.

(THEODORE chuckles.)

THEODORE: The better to bite you with, my dear.

(THEODORE snaps at RICKY. Beat. He chuckles again. Lights fade to kitchen. BEASLEY, JUNE, LUCY, RICCARDO, and WARD.)

BEASLEY: Perhaps we should have some prayer.

JUNE: I don't want prayer.

WARD: That would be nice.

JUNE: I just said I don't want any prayer. Are you crazy? Deaf, maybe?

WARD: You need to calm down, June.

(Beat. JUNE looks at WARD.)

JUNE: All right. Lets do the Lord's Prayer. *(She begins to recite the Lord's Prayer very rapidly, very clipped.)* Our father who art in heaven, hollow be thy name. Thy kingdom come, thy will be done, on earth as it is in heaven. Give us this day our daily bread and forgive

us our trespasses. As we forgive those who trespass
against us. And lead us not into temptation, but deliver
us from evil. For Thine is the kingdom and the power
and the glory, forever. Amen.

JUNE: Oh good, I feel better already. Now the twenty-
third psalm.

WARD: June—

JUNE: *(Recites it very rapidly again. And again, everyone
tries to keep up with her.)* The Lord is my shepherd. I
shall not want. He maketh me to lie down in green
pastures. He leadeth me beside the still waters. He
restoreth my soul. Yea, tho I walk through the valley
of the shadow of death, I will fear no evil. For Thou art
with me. Thy rod and Thy staff, they comfort me. And
I will dwell in the house of the Lord forever.

JUNE: I love that so and now I feel so much better.
How about the Apostles Creed? *(Again she recites very
rapidly.)* I believe in God the Father almight, maker
of heaven and earth. And in Jesus Christ, our only
son and Lord. Who was conceived by the Holy Spirit,
suffered under Pontius Pilate, was crucified dead
and buried. He descended into hell. On the third
day, he rose again from the dead. He ascended into
heaven and sitteth on the right hand of God the father
almighty. From thence he shall judge the quick and
the dead. I believe in the Holy Christian Church, the
communion of saints. The forgiveness of sins and the
life everlasting.

BEASLEY: Mrs Cleaver—

(JUNE *continues to recite above.*)

JUNE: Now everybody!! *(She finishes the creed. Beat. She
looks at them.)*

JUNE: *(Holding her hand straight out in front of her)* Now see how calm I am. You can go home now, Reverend Beasley. You've been a great, great help.

BEASLEY: You don't seem—

JUNE: *(Holding her hand out again)* My hand, Reverend Beasley. You may go.

(BEASLEY *looks at* WARD.)

BEASLEY: If you need anything—

JUNE: How about the words to *Amazing Grace*?

(JUNE *chuckles.* BEASLEY *leaves. She looks at* WARD. *Then, very slowly, begins to sing.*)

JUNE: *(Snapping fingers and singing)* Come on along, and lets get happy. We're gonna chase all the clouds away. *(Spoken)* Now everybody.

(*Fade to* OPIE *and* EDDIE.)

EDDIE: So your father's a sheriff, huh?

OPIE: Yes sir, he is.

EDDIE: So then you'll know what a statement is.

OPIE: I'm sorry?

EDDIE: Confession. Willful endangerment, disturbance of the peace. Ready to talk?

OPIE: Well, I—

EDDIE: I said are you ready to talk?

OPIE: What do you—

EDDIE: Because if you're not, I can always take to beating the hell out of you. It's a thing we practice in this part of the country—beating up fags.

OPIE: It's a thing they practice everywhere.

EDDIE: But I bet we do it best. *(Beat)* You ready to talk?

OPIE: I'm ready.

EDDIE: *(With cassette)* Then start talking.

OPIE: Well...when we found out we were sick, the same day, the same doctor, Ted, Beaver decided we should pay one last visit to our boyhood homes. I told him I could never see Pa again. That it was too painful for both of us. Pa never got over my being gay and I have never really recovered from loosing the biggest part of his love. But I told Ted that I would like for him to see Mayberry, that I'd like to take him on a tour of the place because whether we like it or not, our hometown really defines who we are in the core, you know what I'm saying? So we decided to drive through Mayberry at night, early morning really when no one would be up and the town would be dead and silent and safe. And that's what we did. I showed him the downtown area, my schools, the houses with neighbors who at one time thought the world of me. When Ted asked to be taken by Pa's house, I couldn't tell him where it was at. It was like I'd had some kind of amnesia— memory loss and as we drove around I could feel myself shake inside because I just knew we were going to run into it and that it would be more than I could stand...and we did, finally...and I started to cry...and I started to shake...and when we pulled the car up in the front of the house for a very brief second, I had this overwhelming need to just reach out and take the whole place into my arms, to lay my head on the porch step, to sleep in Aunt Bee's flowers. Then a light went on in Pa's bedroom and we drove off in the car—a rental, a big Buick Le Sabre. A real nice, quiet car with tinted windows...where I couldn't hear a thing, see a thing, want or need anything...and so we came here.

(Pause as EDDIE *looks at* OPIE.*)*

EDDIE: Boo hoo hoo. Now lets start over again. And this time, leave out the shit about Aunt Bee.

(He chuckles as lights fade to the Cleaver home.)

JUNE: *(Angrily)* You expect me to do everything!

RICCARDO: She needs a see-key-a-tree!!

JUNE: And when I'm upset, you try to put me in some kind of a religious trance.

LUCY: Honey—

WARD: I can't talk to her.

RICCARDO: She needs to talk to a see-key-a-tree!!

LUCY: Ricky, why don't you and Ward...

(RICCARDO looks at her. Then gets it and—)

RICCARDO: Ohhh! That's right. Come with me, partner.

WARD: June—

JUNE: Don't expect me to be here when you come back.

LUCY: You boys get out of here now.

(RICCARDO and WARD go. Pause)

LUCY: You've really got the neighbors talking with this crazy act.

JUNE: Not those awful Simpson people.

LUCY: She can't keep her nose out of the window.

JUNE: She's disgusting.

LUCY: And that hair!

JUNE: I know! It's blue!!!

(LUCY and JUNE chuckle. Pause)

LUCY: You know when I left Ricky?

JUNE: I remember.

LUCY: It was the best thing I ever did. Taught him a lesson. Oh, I know, he's still a loud mouth son of a bitch with as much talent as a dancing enchilada, but he's good to me now—and he was good to Little Ricky. And you know how I did it?

JUNE: No.

LUCY: I told him flat out that if he ever touched me or Little Ricky again, I'd shoot him dead. Look at this. *(From her small handbag, she pulls out a tiny gun.)*

JUNE: Lucy!!

LUCY: You'd be surprised how much this does for straightening a man out. *(Whispering)* It's not even loaded, but if he ever gets on my nerves, I just take it out and wave it around a little.

(JUNE and LUCY laugh. Beat)

LUCY: I'm telling you this for an important reason, June. That year when I was gone, I nearly went crazy myself. And you know why?

JUNE: No.

LUCY: Because the person I loved most in the world was still back here and I missed her terribly.

JUNE: Me?

LUCY: You.

(They take hands.)

LUCY: We gotta stick together, honey. Forget the neighbors for a minute. Forget about Ward and all those asshole straight men. What do you want? What can I do for you, June?

JUNE: Tell Ward...to bring Beaver home.

(Fade to THEODORE and BEAVER.)

THEODORE: So do you think of me?

RICKY: I think of you.

THEODORE: Good. You're sort of my living memorial in the straight world.

RICKY: Oh.

(*Beat*)

THEODORE: Are you happy?

RICKY: I'm okay.

THEODORE: But not happy.

RICKY: I'm okay...you're the only guy...you're the only guy I ever did anything with.

THEODORE: Really?

RICKY: Yes.

THEODORE: And why are you telling me this?

RICKY: So you'll know, that's all. I'm not gay. I ain't gay.

THEODORE: Good for you.

(*Beat*)

RICKY: I didn't love you, by the way. So don't think I did, because I didn't.

THEODORE: And don't think I didn't, because I did.

(EDDIE *enters.*)

EDDIE: Hey, Beav, your Dad and brother's here to post bail.

(WARD *and* WALLY *come into the light.*)

WARD: Can you leave us alone for a minute, Eddie?

EDDIE: You want me to leave you alone for a minute, Mister Cleaver?

WARD: If you wouldn't mind.

EDDIE: I don't mind.... Sorry about this, Mister Cleaver. You were always a very nice family. How you doing, Wally? Your old lady come back home, yet?

WALLY: No.

EDDIE: Don't feel too bad. I'm going through the same shit—sorry, Mister Cleaver.

WALLY: Would you mind leaving, Eddie?

EDDIE: Sure thing. *(He exits.)*

WALLY: How you doing, Beav?

THEODORE: Okay. Have you seen Opie?

WALLY: We're gonna bail him out, too. Don't worry.

THEODORE: I'll pay you back...Dad, I'll pay you back.

(WARD comes up to THEODORE and slaps him hard across the face.)

WALLY: Dad!

WARD: That's all I wanted to do. I wanted to come down here, pay your bail and slap you hard across the face.

THEODORE: *(Who has jumped up from seat, ready to square off)* So you did that. So now you can leave.

WALLY: He didn't mean it. Mom's upset and he—

WARD: I meant it!

WALLY: You didn't!

WARD: I did!

WALLY: I know you didn't, Dad.

WARD: If you could see you mother!

WALLY: He didn't!

WARD: What this has done!

THEODORE: *(Overlapping with above)* I'll leave, all right? All right?

(WARD puts his face in his hands.)

WALLY: Dad...Dad...

THEODORE: Dad...

WALLY & THEODORE: Dad...Dad...

WARD: I didn't mean that.

WALLY: He didn't mean that, Beav.

WARD: I didn't mean that.

WALLY: He didn't. Dad—

WARD: I love you.

WALLY: He loves you, Beav.

WARD: *(Weeping)* I love you, but your mom—

WALLY: *(Also crying)* Mom loves you, too. I love you.

THEODORE: Okay.

WARD: But what you did!

WALLY: It was stupid, Beav.

WARD: What you did humiliated us—

WALLY: You shouldn't have done it—

THEODORE: *(Also crying)* Okay.

WARD: We love you and you should come home.

WALLY: Right now, Beav.

THEODORE: I didn't think you'd come.

WARD: You were wrong.

WALLY: You were wrong, Beav.

WARD: Right now, come home.

THEODORE: Okay. Okay.

(No one touches. They just cry and move awkwardly out as the scene fades. We hear a couple of T V commercials. Music lead in and then announcement.)

ANNOUNCER: What do you do when you discover your son is gay? That's today's topic as we visit the home of a once typical American family here on—

AUDIENCE: TELL IT TO JOHNNY!

(Music as lights come up on Cleaver kitchen. WARD. THEODORE, JUNE, OPIE,*and* WALLY *all sit at the table.* JOHNNY *sits between them.)*

JOHNNY: *(Very seriously)* Good morning and welcome to today's show. What do you do when you find out your son is gay? Think about it? What do you do? June—can I call you June?

JUNE: Of course.

JOHNNY: What did you do, June, when you found out that the Beaver was gay.

JUNE: I cried a lot.

JOHNNY: I'll bet. And you, Ward—can I call you Ward?

WARD: Ward is okay.

JOHNNY: What did you do?

WARD: I tried to understand.

JUNE: We both tried to understand.

WARD: We both did, yes.

JOHNNY: But you got very depressed, am I right, June?

JUNE: You can call me June.

JOHNNY: You got very depressed?

JUNE: Yes.

JOHNNY: And what happened?

JUNE: One morning, I took off all my clothes, lay down in the middle of a busy street near our house, and waited for a bus to run over me.

JOHNNY: What a story.

JUNE: But I'm better now.

(Audience applause)

JOHNNY: That's right, that's right. The typical American family finds out that their son is gay, what do they do? And you, Wally—

WALLY: You can call me Wally.

JOHNNY: You look like the strong, sort of macho-type.

WALLY: Sort of.

JOHNNY: What did you do when you found out your brother was gay?

WALLY: I just figured that if that's the way it was, then that's the way it was.

(*Audience applause*)

WALLY: I mean, geesh, when I was in Viet Nam, guys were going down on each other all the time—

(*The audience gasps.*)

JOHNNY: (*Trying to recover*) So Beaver—I can call you Beaver, right?

THEODORE: I'd rather you called me by my real name, Theodore.

JOHNNY: Theodore.

THEODORE: Yes.

JOHNNY: So Theodore, you were caught kissing Little Ricky, am I right?

THEODORE: That's right.

JOHNNY: And then you tried to commit suicide?

THEODORE: Yes.

JOHNNY: And why did you do that?

THEODORE: Because I knew the world hated me—

JOHNNY: The world?

THEODORE: And I thought my parents hated me and I thought that if my parents hated me then what was the point.

JOHNNY: This is your lover, Opie?

THEODORE: Yes.

JOHNNY: *(To audience)* Ladies and Gentlemen, meet Theodore's lover.

(Applause)

JOHNNY: How long have the two of you been together?

OPIE: Only a short time.

JOHNNY: And the sad case of it is, you both have the AIDS virus, am I correct?

OPIE: That's correct.

JOHNNY: So...what does that...feel like to you?

OPIE: I'm angry. I'm pissed.

JOHNNY: *(To* WARD *and* JUNE*)* How have you dealt with the idea that your son and his lover will most probably die before you?

THEODORE: Lots of people are living long productive lives with AIDS.

OPIE: That's right!

(Beat)

WARD: Go on and show them, dear.

JUNE: I keep a scrapbook. I have it here.

JOHNNY: Can we take a look at it?

JUNE: Of course. *(As* JOHNNY *takes the scrapbook)* These are all the articles I can find on AIDS. I don't know why...

WARD: We thought—

JUNE: Yes, we both thought that keeping this might in some way...

JOHNNY: Sure.

JUNE: There are two articles today. This one talks about a possible cure.

JOHNNY: A cure?

JUNE: Maybe. They're not sure. The problem is that the world is run by lazy bureaucrats, racist hate mongers and religious zealots who would rather see minorities and people of color exterminated by a plague of mythic proportions—

WARD: You can tell my wife has become a real radical.

JOHNNY: *(To audience)* And more power to her!!!!

(Applause)

JOHNNY: A mother's love, right here, folks. A mother's desperate search for the life of her son.

WARD: And father's.

THEODORE: And all of us.

JUNE: I've underlined the words hope and promising every time it shows up. *(Reading)* "Hope." "Promising." "Hope." "Hope." "Hoping." "Promising." "As hoped." "Staggering." Now why did I underline...

JOHNNY: A family comes together. A mother's love. A father's love. A scrapbook. And AIDS. Ladies and Gentlemen, you are about to witness an historic event today on *Tell It To Johnny*. Right here in the Cleaver kitchen, the marriage of Beaver and Opie.

(Gasps and then applause.)

JOHNNY: *(Over applause)* As they proclaim their love for one another on national tv.

(Applause swells.)

JOHNNY: Yes! Look at Mrs Cleaver, she's crying.

(*More applause*)

JOHNNY: His own brother will be best man, Wally.

(*Applause*)

JOHNNY: His father will give away the...

WARD: The son.

JOHNNY: And look who's here! Your best friends, the Riccardos!!

(*The* RICCARDOS *come on stage.*)

JOHNNY: There we go! And it's about time, isn't it?

(*More applause*)

JOHNNY: So I understand you've written your own vows.

THEODORE: That's right.

JOHNNY: Why, Theodore? Why, Opie? Why do this on national tv?

THEODORE: Because we have a fucking right—

OPIE: I think it will be clear in the vows we've written. Mister Cleaver? Mrs Cleaver? Wally?

(*They all stand.* OPIE *and* THEODORE *in the center.*)

THEODORE: Everybody loved me when I was a little boy—

OPIE: Even though I knew somehow there was something different about me.

THEODORE: When I found out what it was—

OPIE: Everybody still loved me.

THEODORE: But I knew that if they heard my secret—

OPIE: they would hate me and look down on me.

THEODORE: And so I became an even better little boy—

OPIE: An even better little teenager.

THEODORE: And I hid who I was—

OPIE: Because we feared for our spirit, our hope and our lives.

THEODORE: Now I am a man and part of being a man—

OPIE: Is becoming better and richer in soul.

THEODORE: And so I will not be frightened—

OPIE: And depressed and guilty any longer.

THEODORE & OPIE: There is nothing wrong with the love I feel for you and when I hold you in my arms and when I kiss your lips and your body, I will do so with the utmost respect for who you are and for what you want to be, what you can be with me.

OPIE: No more guilt. No more hidden faces. No more loneliness.

THEODORE: We stand up.

OPIE: We stand up....I love you.

THEODORE: I love you.

OPIE & THEODORE: America, tis of thee.

(OPIE *and* THEODORE *kiss, then...*)

THEODORE: Oh wow. OH Wow! This is like the best thing that's ever happened to me!

(OPIE *and* THEODORE *kiss again as...*)

JOHNNY: *(Very enthusiastically)* Ladies and gentlemen, I present to you, Theodore and Opie Taylor-Cleaver, partners in life!!

LUCY: And I think Ricky should be the first one to kiss the brides!!

(*Much applause and laughter as* LUCY *leads* RICCARDO *up to* THEODORE *and* OPIE. *He hesitates and then* OPIE *and*

Theodore *surround him and kiss both cheeks. A huge, good-natured reaction from* Riccardo.)

Johnny: Thank you, Opie. Thank you, Theodore. And good night, everyone!

Everyone: Goodnight!

(*Music. The music swells. Much applause, confetti as the cast gather around* Opie *and* Theodore. *The lights fade.*)

END OF PLAY